P9-CND-978

DISCARDED

GAYLORD F

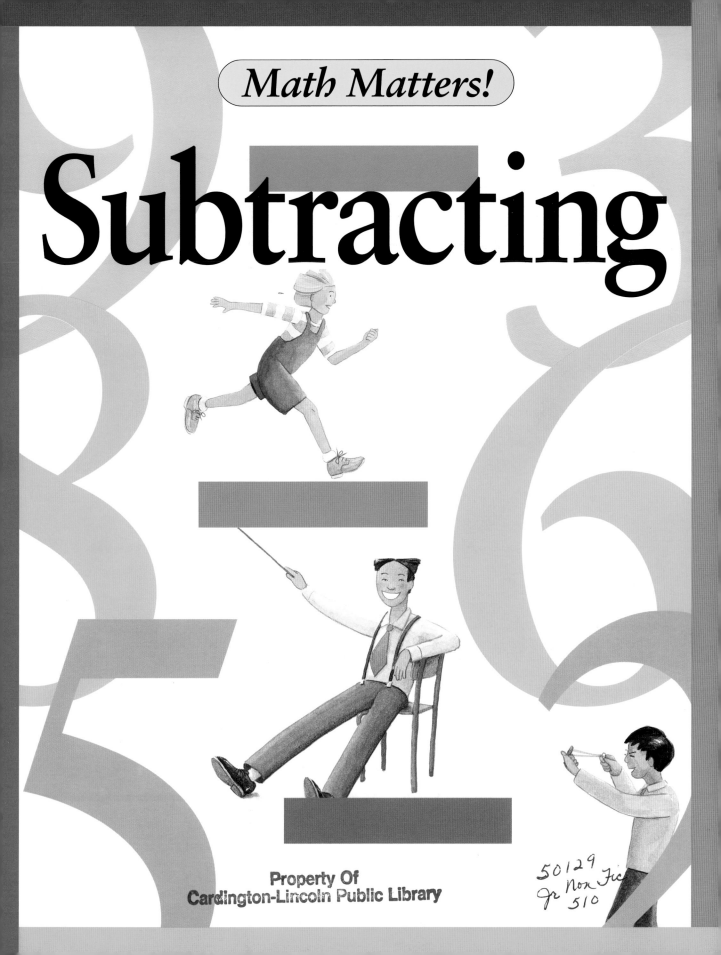

Subtracting

Property Of
Cardington-Lincoln Public Library

50129
Jr Non Fic
510

Look out for these sections to help you learn more about each topic:

Remember...
This provides a summary of the key concept(s) on each two-page entry. Use it to revise what you have learned.

Word check
These are new and important words that help you understand the ideas presented on each two-page entry.

All of the word check entries in this book are shown in the glossary on page 45. The versions in the glossary are sometimes more extensive explanations.

Book link...
Although this book can be used on its own, other titles in the *Math Matters!* set may provide more information on certain topics. This section tells you which other titles to refer to.

Place value
To make it easy for you to see exactly what we are doing, you will find colored columns behind the numbers in all the examples on this and the following pages. This is what the colors mean:

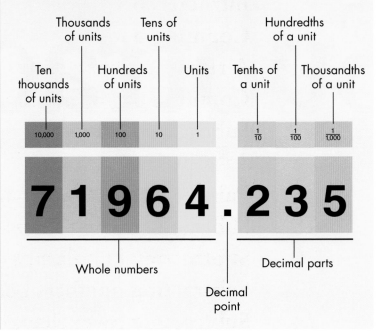

Ten thousands of units — Thousands of units — Hundreds of units — Tens of units — Units — Tenths of a unit — Hundredths of a unit — Thousandths of a unit

10,000 1,000 100 10 1 $\frac{1}{10}$ $\frac{1}{100}$ $\frac{1}{1,000}$

$7\,1\,9\,6\,4\,.\,2\,3\,5$

Whole numbers — Decimal point — Decimal parts

Series concept by *Brian Knapp and Duncan McCrae*
Text contributed by *Brian Knapp and Colin Bass*
Design and production by *Duncan McCrae*
Illustrations of characters by *Nicolas Debon*
Digital illustrations by *David Woodroffe*
Other illustrations by *Peter Bull Art Studio*
Editing by *Lorna Gilbert and Barbara Carragher*
Layout by *Duncan McCrae and Mark Palmer*
Reprographics by *Global Colour*
Printed and bound by *LEGO SpA, Italy*

First Published in the United States in 1999 by Grolier Educational, Sherman Turnpike, Danbury, CT 06816

Copyright © 1999
Atlantic Europe Publishing Company Limited

All rights reserved. No part of this publication may be reproduced, stored in a retrieval system, or transmitted in any form or by any means – electronic, mechanical, photocopying, recording, or otherwise – without prior permission of the Publisher.

Library of Congress Cataloging-in-Publication Data
Math Matters!
    p. cm.
    Includes indexes.
    Contents: v.1.Numbers — v.2.Adding — v.3.Subtracting — v.4.Multiplying — v.5.Dividing — v.6.Decimals — v.7.Fractions – v.8.Shape — v.9.Size — v.10.Tables and Charts — v.11.Grids and Graphs — v.12.Chance and Average — v.13.Mental Arithmetic
ISBN 0–7172–9294–0 (set: alk. paper). — ISBN 0–7172–9295–9 (v.1: alk. paper). — ISBN 0–7172–9296–7 (v.2: alk. paper). — ISBN 0–7172–9297–5 (v.3: alk. paper). — ISBN 0–7172–9298–3 (v.4: alk. paper). — ISBN 0–7172–9299–1 (v.5: alk. paper). — ISBN 0–7172–9300–9 (v.6: alk. paper). — ISBN 0–7172–9301–7 (v.7: alk. paper). — ISBN 0–7172–9302–5 (v.8: alk. paper). — ISBN 0–7172–9303–3 (v.9: alk. paper). — ISBN 0–7172–9304–1 (v.10: alk. paper). — ISBN 0–7172–9305–X (v.11: alk. paper). — ISBN 0–7172–9306–8 (v.12: alk. paper). — ISBN 0–7172–9307–6 (v.13: alk. paper).

    1. Mathematics — Juvenile literature. [1. Mathematics.] I. Grolier Educational Corporation.
QA40.5.M38   1998
510 — dc21   98–7404
                                          CIP
                                          AC

This book is manufactured from sustainable managed forests. For every tree cut down at least one more is planted.

Contents

Introduction

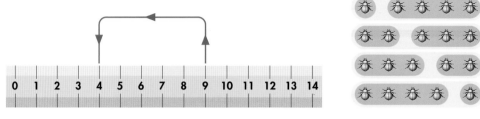

$$1.0 - 0.9 = ?$$

$$\begin{array}{r} 1.\overset{1}{0} \\ -\ \overset{1}{\cancel{0}}.9 \\ \hline 0.1 \end{array}$$

Subtracting is taking away. It is all about separating a large thing into smaller things. We might, for example, know that we have **56** special stamps, but if we sell **23** of them, how many are left in our collection?

Subtraction words include "how many remain?" or "how many are left?" or "what is the difference?" or "how many more?" or even – and you may need to think hard about this one – "what is the amount to be added?"

Subtraction has an enormous range of uses, as you will find in this book. For example, it is used throughout our lives for sorting out home finances. For example, <u>how much</u> money do we <u>have left</u> for the rest of the week after

$$\boxed{?} + 5 - 5 = 14 - 5$$

$$\begin{array}{r} 9\,4\overset{1}{\underset{8}{\cancel{3}}}.\overset{1}{5}\,6 \\ -\ \ \ \underset{}{\cancel{3}}7.9\,0 \\ \hline 9\,0\,5.6\,6 \end{array}$$

$$5 + 2 = 7$$

$$7 - 2 = 5$$

$$7 - 5 = 2$$

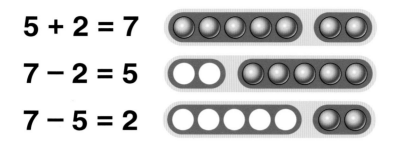

spending money at the store last Saturday?

Sports people use subtracting in working out game scores, timings, and so on (see page 34).

You will find that, by following this book with its stage-by-stage approach, it will be easy to learn the ideas of subtracting. Since each idea is set out on a separate page, you can always refer back to an idea if you temporarily forget it.

As in all of the books in this *Math Matters!* set, there are many examples in this book. They have been designed to be quite varied, because you can use mathematics at any time, any place, anywhere.

$$\frac{3}{4} - \frac{2}{5} = \frac{7}{20}$$

$$238 - 227 = 11$$

Counting back

Counting is simply moving between numbers one at a time. Counting <u>on</u> is a reliable but slow way of adding, and counting <u>back</u> is a slow but reliable way of subtracting.

One use of counting back is the way we use calendars. We may, for example, want to know how much earlier we need to mail a birthday card in order for it to arrive on the actual birthday of a friend or relative. Here is another example.

Counting back for a treat

Jane's mother thought that she would treat the children to a trip to a pantomime in the local theater. The pantomime was to be a Christmas treat. But she found she had to reserve 7 days in advance. She wanted to go to the theatre on December 28th. So she needed to count back 7 days from that day. She used her fingers, as shown on the right.

Jane's mother started on the 28th and, using 7 fingers, she counted back the 7 days.

One day before it would be the 27th.

Two days before it would be the 26th.

Three days before it would be the 25th.

Four days before it would be the 24th.

Five days before it would be the 23rd.

Six days before it would be the 22nd.

Seven days before it would be the 21st.

Counting back with longer numbers

Then Jane's mom discovered that she could get better tickets if they went to the show on the 4th of January and reserved **15** days ahead. So what would be the easiest way to do this?

She decided that it would be easier using a calendar. In this way she soon discovered that she needed to reserve on the **20th** of December.

The shaded area on the calendar shows you how this was done. Remember to start on the 4th of January and count back.

SUN	MON	TUE	WED	THU	FRI	SAT
	1	2	3	4	5	6
7	8	9	10	11	12	13
14	15	16	17	18	19	⟨20⟩
←21	←22	←23	←24	←25	←26	←27
←28	←29	←30	←31			

DECEMBER

JANUARY

SUN	MON	TUE	WED	THU	FRI	SAT
				←1	←2	←3
←⟨4⟩	5	6	7	8	9	10
11	12	13	14	15	16	17
18	19	20	21	22	23	24
25	26	27	28	29	30	31

Remember… Counting back is a slow way of subtracting. Use it only when the numbers are complicated, such as counting back days between months.

Word check

Counting: Finding the total in a set of things by giving each item a number one more than the last one used.

Counting back: Finding the difference within a set of things by going back through the set.

A ruler for subtracting

Subtracting is always the reverse of adding. In adding we put two collections of numbers together. We do this using a plus (+) symbol. In subtraction we take one number from another using a minus (–) symbol.

One way to subtract is to count back using a ruler as a number line. For example, Joan has 9 roses and wants to give 5 to her aunt for a birthday present. How many can she keep for herself?

Step 1: Start at 9.
Step 2: Count back 5.
Step 3: The result is 4.
So, Joan can keep 4 roses for herself.

Step 3: Read the result: 4.

Step 2: Count back by the second number: 5.

Step 1: Put your finger on the first number: 9.

0 1 2 3 4 5 6 7 8 9 10 11 12 13 14

The ruler used as a number line for counting back

One way of showing what we have done is to use words, for example:

Nine take away five leaves four

Or as a word equation:

Nine minus five equals four

And as a number equation this is:

$$9 - 5 = 4$$

Here is a second example, this time with larger numbers:

Giulio wanted to finish making a model building. He was using building blocks. The instructions said he must use **28**. When he counted his stock, he found he had only **12**. How many more should he buy?

This is how Giulio worked it out using a ruler:

Step 1: Start at **28**.
Step 2: Count back **12**.
Step 3: The result is **16**.

He needed to buy sixteen blocks.

Book link… You can find out more about using rulers for adding in the book *Adding* in the *Math Matters!* set.

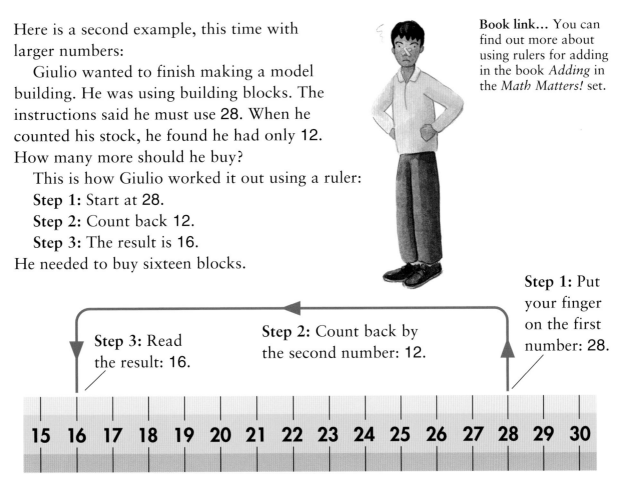

Step 1: Put your finger on the first number: 28.

Step 2: Count back by the second number: 12.

Step 3: Read the result: 16.

15 16 17 18 19 20 21 22 23 24 25 26 27 28 29 30

The ruler used as a number line for counting back

We can write this as:

Twenty-eight take away twelve leaves sixteen

Or as a word equation:

Twenty-eight minus twelve equals sixteen

As a number equation it is:

$28 - 12 = 16$

Remember… A ruler is useful to get you started with subtraction even if you are not good with numbers. Simply follow the three steps shown above.

Word check

+ : The symbol for adding.

− : Between two numbers the symbol means "subtract."

= : The symbol for equals.

Equation: A number sentence using the = symbol, telling us that two different ways of writing a number are the same. For example, 2 + 2 = 4 or 9 − 5 = 4.

Counting on to find the difference

Sometimes you need to count on to find the difference. For example, you will find it is a quick and easy way to count your change.

A book, burger, and fries for Felix

Felix, who lives in San Francisco, was washing his aunt's car. When he finished, she gave him a $10 bill. As it happened, there was a book he wanted that cost $7, so he was going to be able to buy it and still have change for a burger and fries!

He went into the shop, and at the check-out the clerk rang up the cost of the book. Felix handed over the $10 bill.

What she did then was to add to find the difference – that is, the amount of change he was owed. She did it like this:

"Seven," she said, as she put each piece of change in his hand, and then she counted on: "and one is eight, and one more is nine and a final one makes ten."

In this way she could find the change quickly and easily.

Here is the **10** that Felix's aunt gave him:

Here are the **7** that the book cost:

Here are the **3** that Felix received in change:

The clerk had said:

$$7 + 1 + 1 + 1 = 10$$

because she thought that counting on was easier than subtraction. So she gave 3 dollars change, one at a time.

For subtraction she would have had to say:

"I have been given 10, the book cost 7, and so the difference is 3." That is:

$$10 - 7 = 3$$

The clerk was probably right to think that counting on was easier than subtraction, but this was only because the numbers she was using were small. She would have found counting on with larger numbers slow and would have been more likely to make a mistake.

Counting on

These two methods do the same job.

Subtracting

Remember... Counting on is a useful way of subtracting when numbers are small. If you are not confident about getting the right change at a store counter, do what shop assistants do – count on!

Word check
Difference: The result when one number is subtracted from another.

Subtracting rulers

You can use two rulers as number lines to help you subtract. If you put two rulers side by side, you can subtract quite quickly, as you can see in this example.

How far away is it?

Jemma was looking at a road map. Dad had said to her that they were going to drive between Johnston and Charlotteville. Since these were big places, they were each marked with a pin symbol on the map, and the distance was marked in large writing as **28** kilometers.

To get there they had to go through Marytown. The distance from Johnston to Marytown was given as **17** kilometers. But the map did not say how far it was between Marytown and Charlotteville.

Jemma realized she could find the unknown distance using the rulers on her desk. What she needed to do was to take **17** from **28**. Look at the opposite page to see how she did it.

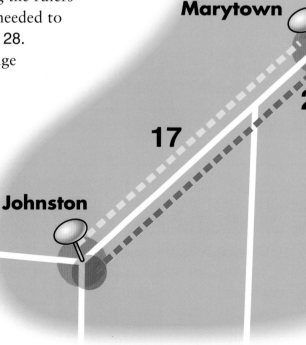

Problem

To subtract 17 from 28 using two rulers.

$$28 - 17 = ?$$

Step 1: Put the 17 of ruler B opposite the 28 of ruler A.

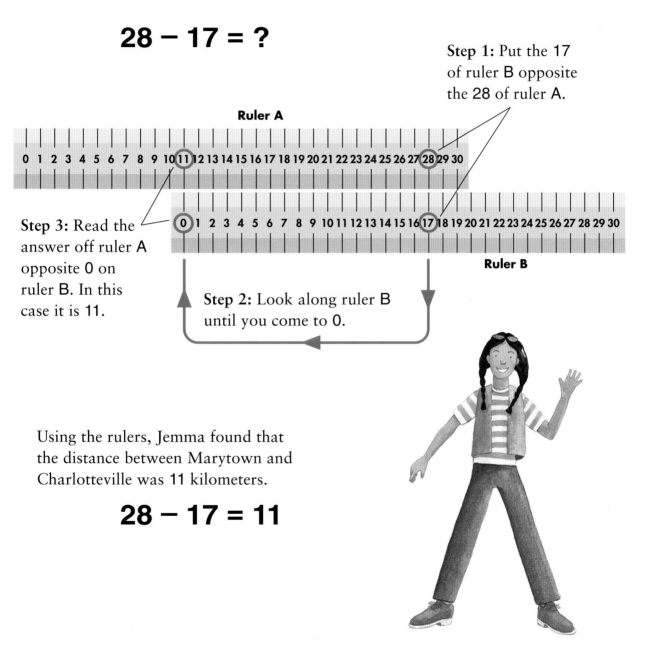

Ruler A

Step 3: Read the answer off ruler A opposite 0 on ruler B. In this case it is 11.

Ruler B

Step 2: Look along ruler B until you come to 0.

Using the rulers, Jemma found that the distance between Marytown and Charlotteville was 11 kilometers.

$$28 - 17 = 11$$

Remember… Subtracting is the reverse of adding.

Book link… Find out more about adding using two rulers in the book *Adding* in the *Math Matters!* set.

Subtracting facts

Subtracting facts are the answers we get when we take one number from another.

Here is a simple way to find out five subtraction facts.

In this case we are using a group of **5** beetles, but you could do this with a group of anything of any size.

Step 1: Put the beetles in a row. This simply makes it easier to see what we are doing.

Step 2: Separate them into two groups. Separating is a way of subtracting, as you will see on page 15.

We might start with a group of blue beetles which will be separated into two groups.

Step 1: The blue beetles are placed in a row.

Step 2: The beetles have now been separated into groups. The numbers tell you how many are in each group. There are five beetles in each of the lines below.

▼ **Read what has happened below. Also, notice that there are many ways to talk about subtracting.**

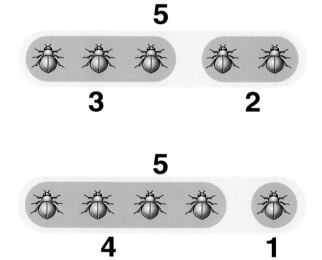

Total
5

1
Group

4
Group

Five minus one leaves four
5 − 1 = 4

5

2 **3**

Taking two from five leaves three
5 − 2 = 3

5

3 **2**

Five take away three leaves two
5 − 3 = 2

5

4 **1**

Five subtract four leaves one
5 − 4 = 1

Remember… There are many ways to talk about how you subtract. If you look at the sentences above, you will see that we have used several different ways. You can use whichever suits you. But notice that in each case the mathematics symbols are all written the same way!

Word check
Minus: Another word meaning "subtract."
Subtracting facts: The answers we work out and remember as a result of subtracting one number from another. For example, 12 − 7 = 5 is a subtracting fact.

Pairs of subtracting facts

You can usually get two subtracting facts from each adding fact by knowing that facts come in families.

You have probably learned your adding facts from the *Adding* book in the *Math Matters!* set. They are easier to learn than subtracting facts. However, you can get two subtracting facts from each adding fact. This is because adding two numbers together in any order gives the same result, but the order in which you subtract numbers gives different results.

If we look at the adding fact:

6 + 3 = 9

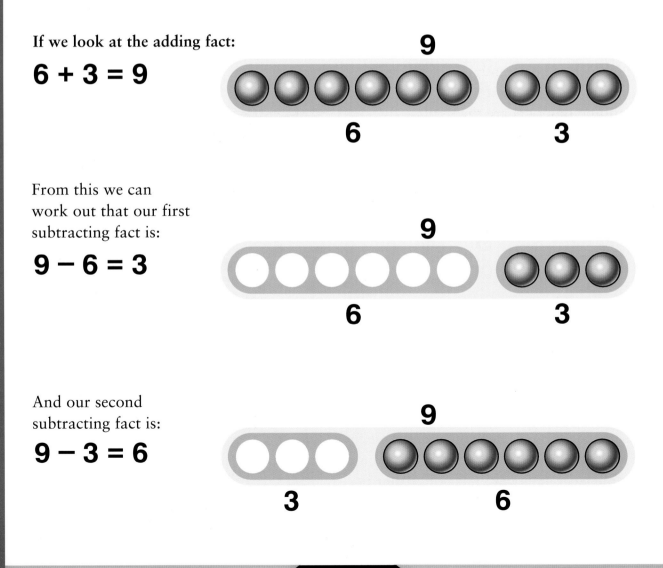

From this we can work out that our first subtracting fact is:

9 − 6 = 3

And our second subtracting fact is:

9 − 3 = 6

Here is another fact family:

5 + 2 = 7

This is our adding fact.

From this we can work out that:

7 − 2 = 5

and

7 − 5 = 2

Below is a fact family with only one subtracting fact because the adding numbers are the same:

4 + 4 = 8

This is our adding fact.

From this we learn that:

8 − 4 = 4

and

8 − 4 = 4

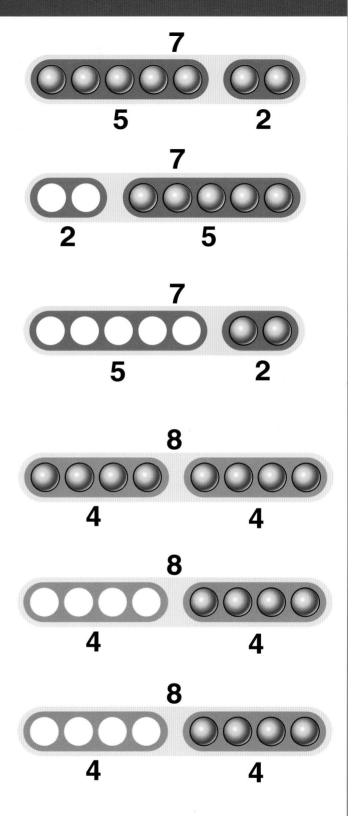

Remember... The order in which you do your subtracting is important

Word check
Fact family: A group of related facts about adding and subtracting or about multiplying and dividing.

Subtracting using shapes

If you are not sure how to subtract, then one way is to lay out the problem as a model, using mathematical shapes.

As numbers get bigger, they can be more difficult to work with. Here are some examples of how shapes can be used to find answers. You might want to make your own shapes from paper to work out other problems.

◄ This is a shape for 100. You can prove this by counting up all 100 squares, or units, if you like. Some people call this shape a <u>flat</u>.

◄ This is a shape for 10. Some people call this a <u>long</u>. Ten longs make a flat.

◄ This is a shape for 1. It can also be called a <u>unit</u>. Ten units make a long.

Subtracting **4** from **9** using shapes: **9 − 4 = ?**

Step 1: We lay out 9 as units.

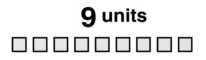

9 units

Step 2: We subtract the 4 units.

4 units

Step 3: Then we count up the units that are left. The answer is 5 units.

5 units

Word check

Flat: A large square representing 100. It can also be made up of ten "longs" put side by side.

Long: A long shape representing 10.

Unit: 1 of something. A small, square shape representing 1.

We can also use the shapes to work with bigger numbers.

Subtracting **227** from **238** using shapes: **238 − 227 = ?**

Step 1: Set out **238** as **2** flats, **3** longs, and **8** units.

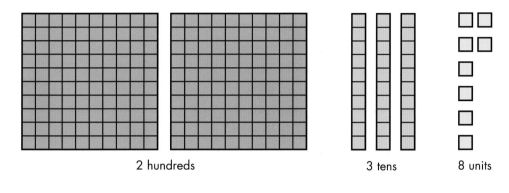

2 hundreds   3 tens   8 units

Step 2: Subtract **227** as **2** flats, **2** longs, and **7** units.

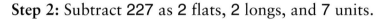
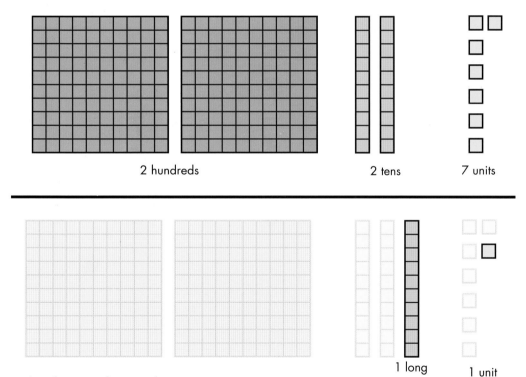

2 hundreds   2 tens   7 units

1 long   1 unit

Step 3: As shown above, there are two flats in each case, so they cancel out. Two longs and seven units can also be taken away. The amount that is left over is **1** long and **1** unit, or **11**.

238 − 227 = 11

Remember... The rule is to subtract units from units, tens from tens, and hundreds from hundreds. Now turn the page to see another way of subtracting.

Subtracting in columns

Most people subtract numbers by first placing one below the other in columns.

The number you are subtracting from should be at the top, while the number you are going to subtract from it is written below.

You must also make sure that the numbers are lined up in columns. In this book, as with others in the *Math Matters!* set, the columns are shown in color, as on this page (see page 2 for more help with colored columns).

Start by looking at the difference between two single-digit numbers. The problem shown below is 7 − 4 = 3.

This is the problem set out in a column.

This yellow-colored column is used to make sure that all the numbers stay exactly below each other. You will see how important this is when we subtract large numbers from one another.

Units

7
−
4
=
3

This is the equation written out in a row.

7 − 4 = 3

Units

7
−
4
=
3

Units

7
− 4
―――
3

When subtracting is done in columns, the = sign is replaced by a single line.

These are the units shown as shapes to help you see what is happening.

7 − 4 = 3

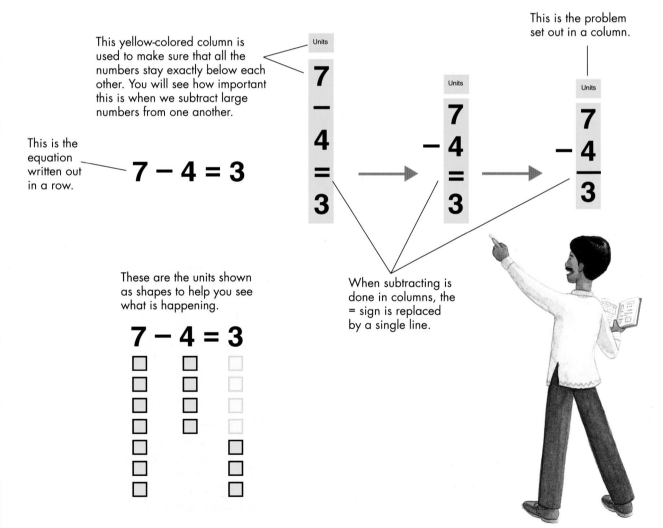

Here are some further examples of subtracting single digits.

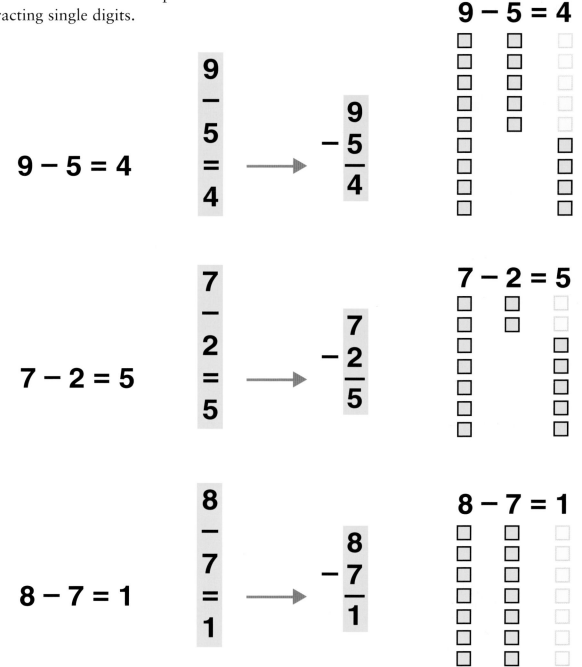

$$9 - 5 = 4$$

$$7 - 2 = 5$$

$$8 - 7 = 1$$

Remember... The key to success when subtracting is to keep all of your numbers in columns. This is the same idea used in adding, and it becomes very important as the numbers get bigger, as we shall soon see.

Word check
Digit: The numerals 1, 2, 3, 4, 5, 6, 7, 8, 9, or 0. Several may be used to stand for a larger number.
Single-digit number: A number between 0 and 9.

Subtracting numbers between 10 and 99

When subtraction includes numbers between **10** and **99**, you have to use two columns to find your answer.

Once again put the number you are starting from on top and the one you are subtracting below it. It is very important that you line them up on the right in columns. As before, draw a line underneath these numbers to replace the equals symbol. Then you can subtract in each column starting on the right.

First, let's subtract a single-digit number from a two-digit number, such as:

$$16 - 5 = ?$$

Two-digit number   Single-digit number

This is done using columns as follows:

Step 1: Line up the numbers to the right.

Step 2: We begin on the <u>right</u>. We take away the number on the second line from the number on the top line: $6 - 5 = 1$.
   Put 1 below the line in the units column.

Step 3: There are no tens in the second number, so the answer in the tens column is $1 - 0 = 1$. Write 1 below the line in the tens column to give the answer: **11**.

These are the tens and units shown as shapes to help you see what is happening.

16 − 5 = 11

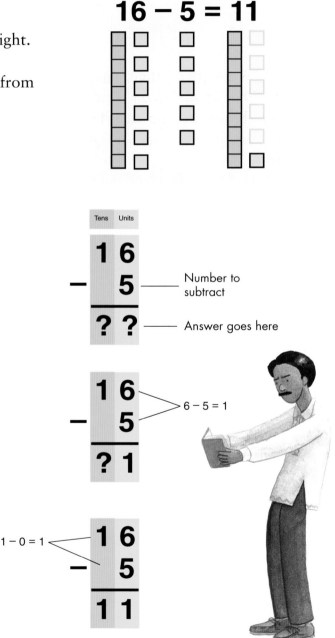

Tens	Units
1	**6**
−	**5**
?	**?**

Number to subtract

Answer goes here

$6 - 5 = 1$

1	**6**
−	**5**
?	**1**

$1 - 0 = 1$

1	**6**
−	**5**
1	**1**

22

Subtracting 21 from 34

In this case we subtract one two-digit number from another:

34 − 21 = ?

Step 1: Line up both sets of numbers on the right.

```
  3 4
− 2 1
─────
  ? ?
```

Step 2: We begin on the <u>right</u>. We take the number on the second line from the number on the top line: 4 − 1 = **3**.

Put **3** below the line in the units column.

```
  3 4
− 2 1        4 − 1 = 3
─────
  ? 3
```

Step 3: Now work on the next column <u>left</u> to deal with the tens. Again, take away: 3 − 2 = **1**.

The 1 is brought down to the answer line, making the final answer **13**.

```
3 − 2 = 1    3 4
           − 2 1
           ─────
             1 3
```

Remember… Follow the rules. Put one number above the other, lining them up on the right using columns. Start subtracting the right-hand numbers, then move to the left a column at a time.

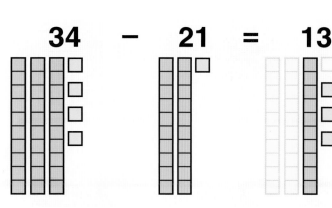

34 − 21 = 13

Word check
Single-digit number: A number between 0 and 9.
Two-digit number: A number between 10 and 99.

Subtracting by exchanging

When the top number is smaller than the bottom number in any column, we cannot subtract in the way shown on previous pages. Instead, we must use either the exchanging or regrouping method.

   This page shows how exchanging works. The <u>alternative</u> "regrouping" method is shown on pages 26 and 27. In both cases we will work out:

34 – 19 = ?

Remember that all numbers are made up of units. So 34 is actually 34 units. We write 3 tens and 4 units as a shorthand, but when subtracting, we can move one set of ten units from the tens column into the units column.

Tens of units	Units
3	**4**
1	**9**
?	**?**

Here is what the number 34 looks like in shapes.

Here is what the number 19 looks like in shapes.

Exchanging

Step 1: To subtract 9 units from 4 units, we have added 10 units to the 4 above, making it 14.
   At the same time, we have added 10 units to the tens column below to balance out what we have done above.

? **?**

Step 2: Now we can take away 9 units from the 14 units to leave 5 units.
   Then we take the 2 tens away from the 3 tens to leave one 10.
   The answer is 15.

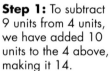
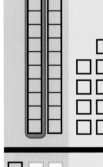
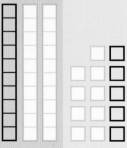

Pen-pal weather

Stephen, who lived in Calgary, Canada, had an e-mail friend, Nopadom, in Bangkok, Thailand.

Stephen and Nopadom were exchanging information about the weather. In August Nopadom e-mailed that the temperature was 34°C. Stephen e-mailed to say that in Calgary it had just reached 19°C. So how much warmer was it in Bangkok?

$$34 - 19 = ?$$

Step 1: Put the number you are subtracting below the one you are subtracting from, line them up on the right, and draw a line underneath them.

Step 2: Begin in the units column: 4 − 9 = ?

Since 9 is bigger than 4, we need to add to the 4. Here we <u>exchange</u> 10 units from the column to the left. Write a 1 beside the 4 to show that it is now 14, and cross out the 1 in the second row of the tens column, adding 1 (1 + 1 = 2) and writing 2 to balance the 10 units we have exchanged. We can now subtract in the units column: 14 − 9 = **5**. Write the 5 below the line.

Step 3: Move left to the tens column.

Subtracting gives us 3 − 2 = **1**, which we write below the line.

It was **15**°C warmer in Bangkok than Calgary!

$$34 - 19 = 15$$

Remember... In the exchanging method we take **1** from the column to the left to use it as **10** at the top of our working column while at the same time <u>adding 1 to the lower number of the column to the left of it</u>.

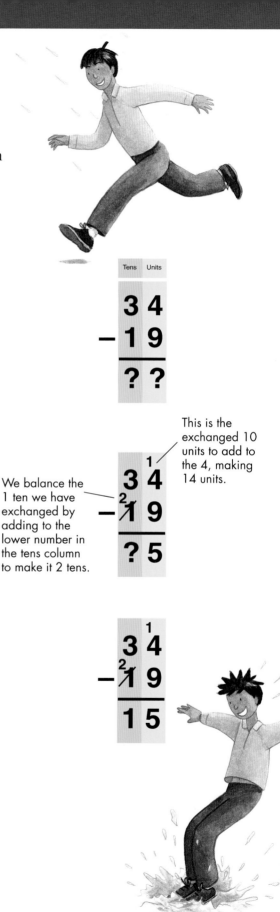

This is the exchanged 10 units to add to the 4, making 14 units.

We balance the 1 ten we have exchanged by adding to the lower number in the tens column to make it 2 tens.

Subtracting by regrouping

You can subtract by the "regrouping" method. This is an <u>alternative</u> to the "exchanging" method shown on pages 24 and 25 using the same numbers.

$$34 - 19 = ?$$

Remember that all numbers are made up of units. So 34 is actually 34 units. We write 3 tens and 4 units as a shorthand, but when subtracting, we can move one set of ten units from the tens column into the units column.

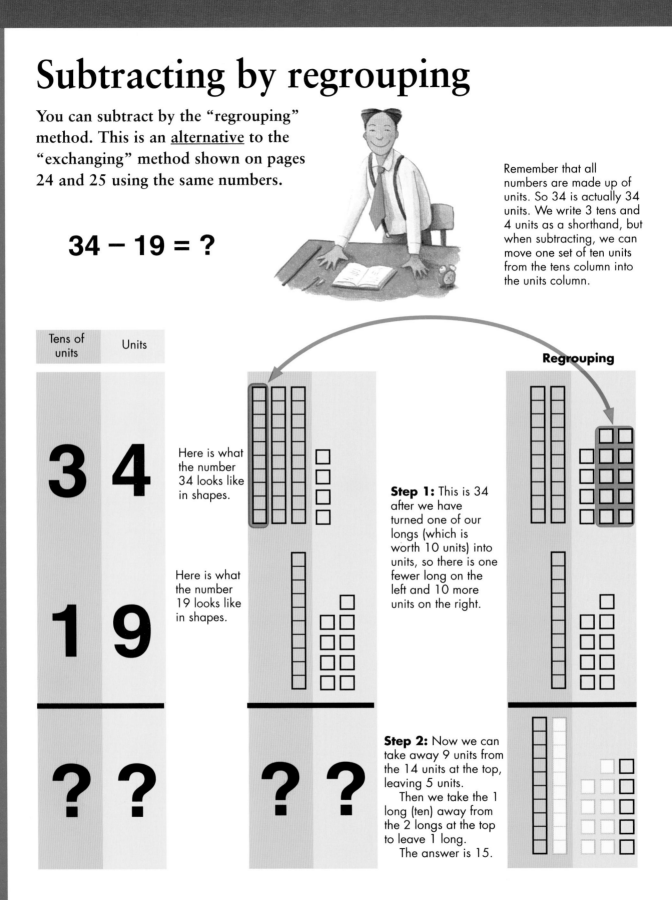

Tens of units	Units
3	**4**
1	**9**
?	**?**

Here is what the number 34 looks like in shapes.

Here is what the number 19 looks like in shapes.

Regrouping

Step 1: This is 34 after we have turned one of our longs (which is worth 10 units) into units, so there is one fewer long on the left and 10 more units on the right.

Step 2: Now we can take away 9 units from the 14 units at the top, leaving 5 units.
   Then we take the 1 long (ten) away from the 2 longs at the top to leave 1 long.
   The answer is 15.

Changes in temperature

Juan's class was studying how much the temperature changed throughout the day. The table on the right shows the results for a school week.

	Highest in °C (maximum)	Lowest in °C (minimum)	Difference
Monday	25	14	11
Tuesday	31	19	12
Wednesday	26	18	8
Thursday	34	19	15
Friday	25	16	9

This is how Juan did the one for Thursday:

$$34 - 19 = ?$$

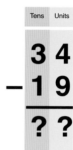

Step 1: Put the number you are subtracting below the one you are subtracting from, line them up on the right in columns, and draw a line underneath them. Now subtract in each column starting on the right.

Step 2: Start with the units column. In this case it is 4 − 9.

Since 9 is bigger than 4, we need to add to the 4. Here we <u>regroup</u> 10 units from the tens column to the left. But because we have regrouped 1 ten from the 3 tens at the top of the column to the left, we reduce the 3 by 1 and write a 2 in its place.

We then write a 1 beside the units column to show that it is now 14 units. Now we can subtract in the units column: 14 − 9 = **5**.

After regrouping there are only 2 tens on this side.

During regrouping 1 ten is transferred to the units column as 10 units. Added to the 4 units already there, this makes a total of 14 units in the units column.

Step 3: Now subtract in the tens column. Remember, we have regrouped a ten, so there are now only 2 tens in the top row of the tens column. Subtracting gives us: 2 − 1 = **1**. The temperature change on Thursday was **15°C**.

$$34 - 19 = 15$$

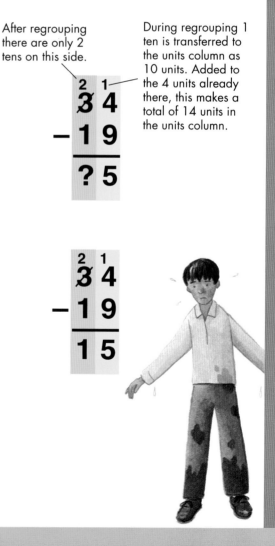

Remember... In the regrouping method we <u>move 1 from the top of the column to the left to use it as 10 at the top of our working column.</u>

Subtracting large numbers

A large number, such as **8,848**, tells you how it is made up when you say it out loud: "eight thousand (**8,000**), eight hundred (**800**), and forty (**40**) eight (**8**)." This number fits across four columns, as shown on the right.

1,000	100	10	1
8	**8**	**4**	**8**

Subtracting large numbers is not difficult. As before, you <u>must</u> organize your numbers into columns and work from right to left, as you will see in the example below.

The world's highest peaks

The world has many high mountains, of which the highest is Mount Everest. The table on the right shows you the ten highest peaks and their height in meters. But how much taller is Mount Everest than the tenth highest mountain, Annapurna?

	Mountain	Height (meters)
1	Everest	**8,848**
2	K-2	**8,611**
3	Kanchenjunga	**8,598**
4	Lhotse	**8,516**
5	Makalu	**8,481**
6	Cho Oyu	**8,201**
7	Dhaulagiri	**8,172**
8	Manaslu	**8,156**
9	Nanga Parbat	**8,126**
10	Annapurna	**8,078**

We need to subtract the height of Annapurna (8,078) from the height of Everest (8,848).

8,848 − 8,078 = ?

Note: This calculation is done using the regrouping method (see page 26).

Steps 1 and 2: Put the number you are subtracting below the one you are subtracting from, line them up on the right in columns, and draw a line underneath them. Now subtract in each column starting on the right.

Start with units: 8 − 8 = **0**. Write the answer below the line.

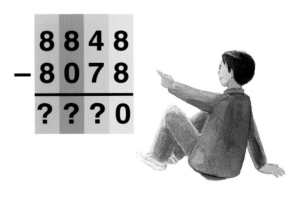

```
  8 8 4 8
− 8 0 7 8
─────────
  ? ? ? 0
```

Step 3: Now subtract the tens. Subtract the next column to the left. Since the 4 at the top is less than 7, we need to regroup **100** from the hundreds column. Since we are working with tens, the regrouping gives us **10 tens** and the 4 tens we already have. The subtraction is now: 14 − 7 = **7**.

```
      7 14
  8 8 4 8
− 8 0 7 8
─────────
  ? ? 7 0
```

Step 4: Now subtract the next column to the left. This is the hundreds column.

Remembering that as we regrouped from this column in step 3, we have reduced the 8 at the top to 7. The subtraction is now: 7 − 0 = **7**.

```
      7 14
  8 8 4 8
− 8 0 7 9
─────────
  ? 7 7 0
```

Step 5: Now subtract thousands. Subtract the next column to the left. This is the thousands column.

The subtraction is: 8 − 8 = **0**.

When a zero is the first number, we normally leave it out, and so in this case we are left with an answer of **770**.

```
      7 14
  8 8 4 8
− 8 0 7 9
─────────
    7 7 0
```

By subtracting, we know that Everest is 770 meters higher than the tenth highest mountain, Annapurna.

Remember… There is no real difference between subtracting with big or small numbers. Just line the numbers up on the right, and subtract starting from the right. You can use either exchanging or regrouping.

Subtracting numbers with zeros

Many numbers contain zero. When you subtract, you treat a zero just like any other number.

How far have we traveled?

Laura and Luke were writing out their vacation diaries. One important thing to note down was the record of how far they had traveled in the car each day. This is what they recorded for the four days of their minibreak:

	The morning of the first day, just before they started (Day 1).	The morning of Day 2, just before they started.	The morning of Day 3, just before they started.	The morning of Day 4, back home.
Distance	**32,990**	**33,124**	**33,492**	**33,805**

To find out how far they had driven over the whole trip, they had to subtract the distance at the start of Day 4 from the distance at the start of Day 1. This is what they did:

33,805 − 32,990 = ?

Note: This calculation is done using the exchanging method. See page 24.

Steps 1 and 2: As before, put the number you are subtracting below the one you are subtracting from. Line them up on the right in columns. You do not need to put commas in your work when subtracting.

Subtract the right-hand column (units) first. 5 − 0 = **5**.

10,000	1,000	100	10	1

```
  3 3 8 0 5
− 3 2 9 9 0
-----------
  ? ? ? ? 5
```

Step 3: Now subtract in the next column to the left, the tens column.

In this case it is 0 − 9, which won't work. Exchange 1 from the hundreds column to make 10 tens. The subtraction is now: 10 − 9 = **1**.

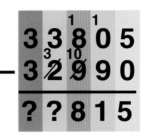

Step 4: Now subtract in the hundreds column.

The lower number is actually 10 because we had to exchange a ten in step 2.

8 − 10 won't go. Exchange 1 from the thousands column to add to the 8 and make 18 hundreds at the top of the hundreds column. The subtraction is now: 18 − 10 = **8**.

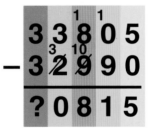

Steps 5 and 6: Move left to the thousands column. Remember we have exchanged a thousand; the subtraction is now: 3 − 3 = **0**.

Subtract the next column to the left. This is the tens of thousands column. The subtraction is again: 3 − 3 = **0**.

We do not write the zeros when they occur at the start of a number, which means that the distance was **815**.

33,805 − 32,990 = 815

Remember... How to work with zeros. When you are subtracting with zeros in the top line, unless the number below it is also zero, you will need to carry a "1" across. Which means 0 becomes 10.

Book link... For more on the use of zeros see the book *Numbers* in the *Math Matters!* set.

Subtracting decimal numbers

Decimals show whole numbers and parts of numbers. A period is placed after the units, so that we will know which one it is. The period is called a decimal point.

Just as with whole numbers, which have the smallest on the right and the largest on the left, every number to the right of the decimal point has a value ten times smaller than its left-hand neighbor. The further it is to the right, the smaller it is. Numbers below units are described as tenths, hundredths, thousandths, and so on.

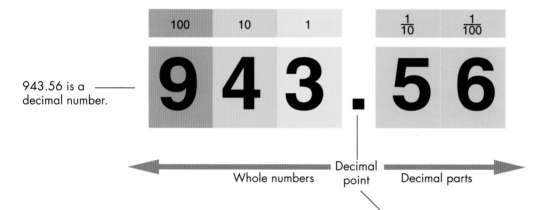

| 100 | 10 | 1 | | $\frac{1}{10}$ | $\frac{1}{100}$ |

9 4 3 . 5 6

943.56 is a decimal number.

← Whole numbers — Decimal point — Decimal parts →

We <u>separate</u> whole numbers from parts of whole numbers using a decimal point.

Subtracting with decimals

Subtracting with decimals is just the same as subtracting with whole numbers. Here are the stages in subtracting the decimal number 37.9 from another decimal number, 943.56:

$943.56 - 37.9 = ?$

Note: This calculation is done using the exchanging method. See page 24.

Step 1: Put the number you are subtracting below the one you are subtracting from, making sure the decimal point lines up. If the numbers have an unequal number of decimals, add extra zeros to fill the columns. In this case a zero (0) has been added to the 37.9 to make it 37.90.

Line up the numbers using the decimal point.

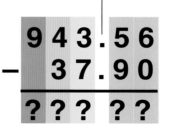

$$
\begin{array}{r}
9\,4\,3\,.\,5\,6 \\
-\quad 3\,7\,.\,9\,0 \\
\hline
?\,?\,?\,.\,?\,? \\
\end{array}
$$

Step 2: Now start subtracting from the right (the hundredths column): 6 − 0 = **6**. Write this below the line in the hundredths column.

$$
\begin{array}{r}
9\ 4\ 3.5\ 6 \\
-\quad 3\ 7.9\ 0 \\
\hline
?\ ?\ ?\ ?\ 6
\end{array}
$$

Steps 3 to 5: In the next column (tenths), 5 − 9 won't work, so exchange 1 from the column to the left, and increase the bottom number by 1. Now it is: 15 − 9 = **6**.

In the next column (units) 3 − 8 (7 + the exchanged 1) won't work, so exchange again from the left: 13 − 8 = **5**.

In the next column (tens) 4 − 4 (3 + the exchanged 1) = **0**.

The last step is 9 − 0 = **9**.

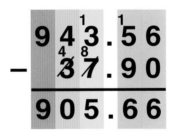

Step 6: Put a decimal point in the answer exactly below the other decimal points. This gives the final answer, which is **905.66**.

Remember... When subtracting decimals, line up the numbers on the decimal point.

Book link... Find out more about decimals in the book *Decimals* in the *Math Matters!* set.

Word check

Decimal number: A number that contains parts of units as well as whole units. The decimal point is used to separate the units from the parts of a unit.

Decimal point: A dot written after the units when a number contains parts of a unit as well as whole numbers.

Subtracting in your head

Many sports and games need quick and accurate use of mathematics. A good example of this is darts.

Usually, each player starts with a score of **501**. The score for each three darts is added up, and then the total is subtracted from the remaining score. The first one to reach zero wins.

In this example we show you how the players used a variety of methods to subtract quickly. Check them for yourself to see which one suits you best.

Each player has three darts, like the ones shown here. The target is a dartboard marked off in numbered zones.

The players take turns standing a fixed distance from the board and throwing their darts into it.

The picture below shows the points system used in darts.

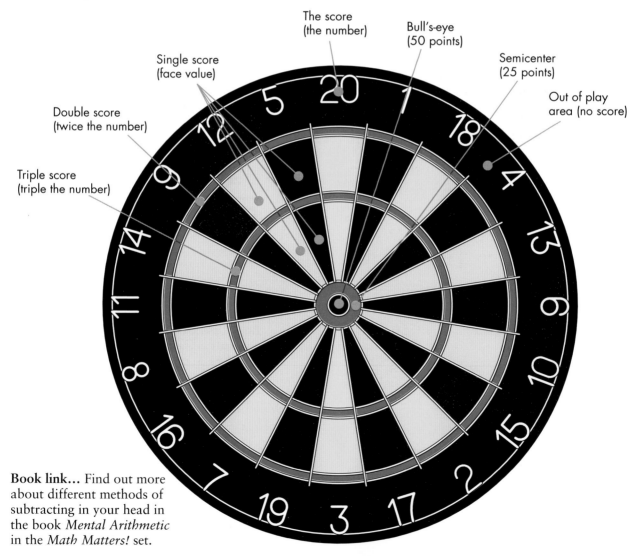

The score (the number)

Bull's-eye (50 points)

Single score (face value)

Semicenter (25 points)

Double score (twice the number)

Out of play area (no score)

Triple score (triple the number)

Book link... Find out more about different methods of subtracting in your head in the book *Mental Arithmetic* in the *Math Matters!* set.

Sara

Starting score: 501

First throw gets a total of: 127

So the score left is:

501 − 127 = 374

We can do this by counting up:
127 + **70** = 197; 197 + **4** = 201;
201 + **300** = 501.
By this method the answer is:
70 + 4 + 300 = 374

Second throw gets a score of: 123

374 − 123 = 251

Do this subtraction by counting up:
123 + **200** = 323; 323 + **50** = 373;
373 + **1** = 374.
By this method the answer is:
200 + 50 + 1 = 251

Third throw gets a score of: 97

251 − 97 = 154

Do this subtraction by subtracting 100
and adding back 3! (−**100** + **3** = 97)
251 − **100** = 151; 151 + **3** = 154.

Fourth throw gets a score of: 154

154 − 154 = 0

So Sara wins!

Nasim

Starting score: 501

First throw gets a total of: 79

So the score left is:

501 − 79 = 422

We can do this subtracting using
the exchanging method:

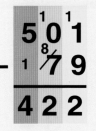

Second throw gets a score of: 147

422 − 147 = 275

Do this subtraction by counting up:
147 + **5** = 152; 152 + **70** = 222;
222 + **200** = 422
By this method the answer is:
5 + 70 + 200 = 275

Third throw gets a score of: 119

275 − 119 = 156

(Do this subtraction by taking off
120 and adding back 1!)

Remember… There are many ways of
subtracting. Learn to use the one that
works most easily for the numbers.

Subtracting and minus numbers

Sometimes when you subtract, the number you are subtracting from is smaller than the number you are subtracting. This is what happens.

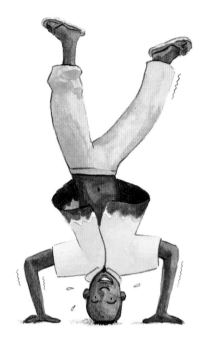

Subtracting above zero

For an ordinary subtraction where the number you are subtracting from is bigger than the number you are subtracting the answer is above zero (0). This can be shown using a number line.

For example: **5 − 3 = ?**

5 is your starting number, and 3 is your journey along the number line. Use the following steps:

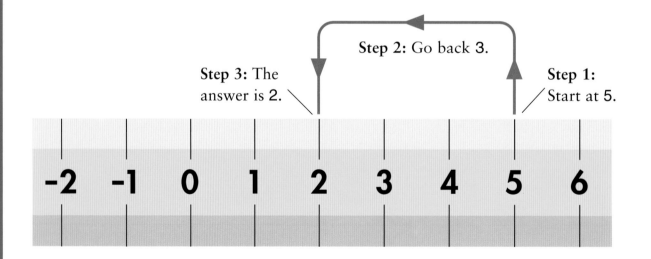

Step 2: Go back 3.

Step 3: The answer is 2.

Step 1: Start at 5.

-2 -1 0 1 2 3 4 5 6

To subtract 3, we travel 3 back (to the left).
The answer is +2, normally just written as "2."

Subtracting below zero

When the number you are subtracting from is smaller than the number you are subtracting, the answer is below zero. This can also be shown using a ruler.

For example: $3 - 5 = ?$

Use the number line again:
3 is your starting number, and 5 is your journey along the ruler. Use the following steps:

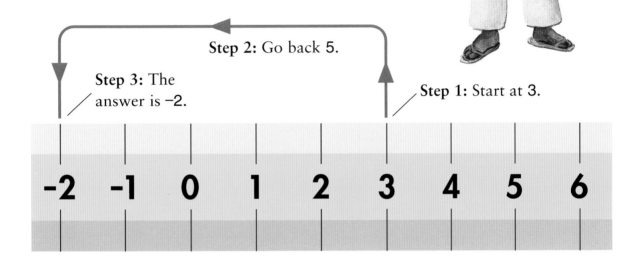

Step 2: Go back 5.

Step 3: The answer is −2.

Step 1: Start at 3.

To subtract 5, we travel 5 to the left. The answer is −2, which we would normally say as "minus 2."

This number is below zero and, like all numbers below zero, is called a minus number. See page 38 for what we mean when subtracting <u>across</u> zero.

Remember... Some subtractions can give minus numbers. Then you must use a minus sign immediately in front of the number.

Word check

− : Between two numbers this symbol means "subtract" or "minus." In front of one number it means the number is a minus number. In Latin *minus* means "less."

Minus numbers: The numbers that fall below zero on a number line (scale). Minus numbers or zero cannot be used for counting, only for measuring things like temperature. Minus numbers are also called negative numbers.

Book link... Find out more about minus numbers in the book *Adding* in the *Math Matters!* set.

Subtracting across zero

A minus number is a number with a minus sign in front of it (see page 37). There are many cases when people need to work with minus numbers. Here is an example.

Falling levels

Reservoirs are used to store water from rivers. Engineers know how much water they want to store in a reservoir. This can be thought of as the normal level. The level of water in a reservoir can be measured with a rod placed beside the dam.

Normal is marked as zero; a scale can then be marked up and down from normal. Numbers above normal are plus numbers; numbers below normal are minus numbers.

At the end of a rainy period an engineer measured the water level in their reservoir as 1.0 meters above normal; but since there was no more rain, he had to release some of the water to keep the river flowing. By the end of a week the water level had fallen to 0.9 meters above normal. How much had the water level fallen?

$$1.0 - 0.9 = ?$$

The answer, 0.1 meters, is shown on the right.

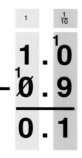

Word check

+ : Between two numbers this symbol means "plus" and is the symbol for adding. In front of one number it means the number is a plus number. In Latin *plus* means "more."

Plus numbers: The numbers that fall above zero on a number line (scale). They are called this to separate them clearly from minus numbers. They are the same as counting numbers. Plus numbers are also called positive numbers.

But at the end of eight weeks without rain, the level of the reservoir had fallen to below normal. The engineers read this as −2.0 meters since it was 2.0 meters below zero. How much had the water level fallen altogether?

To find out, the engineer had to subtract with a minus number. The minus number is shown in parentheses so that you can see it clearly:

1.0 − (−2.0) = ?

First, from the picture of the measuring gauge on the right, you can see the answer must be **3.0** meters.

Subtracting a minus number is the same as adding a plus number:

1.0 − (−2.0) = 1.0 + 2.0 = 3.0

The same rule works for decimal numbers. Suppose the water level had fallen from **1.2** meters to **−2.1** meters. The fall in the water level would be worked out as:

1.2 − (−2.1) = 1.2 + 2.1 = 3.3

You can check this on the gauge, too.

Remember... Subtracting a minus number is the same as adding a plus number.

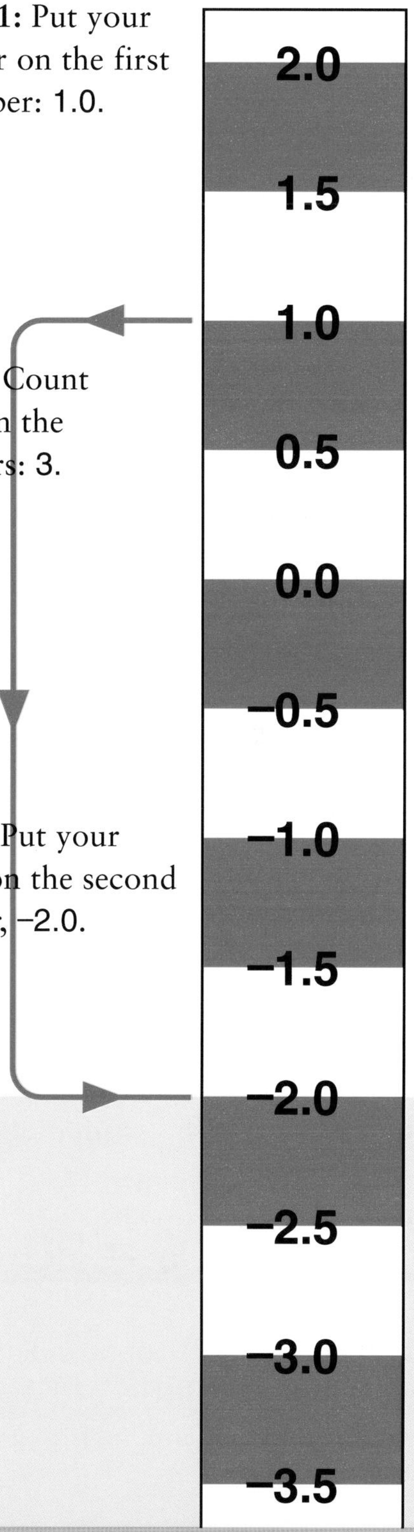

Step 1: Put your finger on the first number: 1.0.

Step 3: Count between the numbers: 3.

Step 2: Put your finger on the second number, −2.0.

2.0
1.5
1.0
0.5
0.0
−0.5
−1.0
−1.5
−2.0
−2.5
−3.0
−3.5

Subtracting fractions

Subtracting fractions is no more difficult than adding them. First, you look to see if they are similar fractions (the bottom numbers of the fractions are the same). To subtract fractions successfully, these numbers must be the same.

For example, ²⁄₄ and ¾ have the same bottom numbers (denominators).

$$\frac{3}{4} - \frac{2}{4} = \frac{1}{4}$$

1 unit

$\frac{1}{4}$

$\frac{3}{4}$

The number of parts we have (also called the numerator)

The number of parts the original was split into (also called the denominator)

Subtracting different kinds of fractions

Often, we want to subtract fractions that have different bottom numbers (they are not similar).

For example: $\frac{3}{4} - \frac{2}{5} = ?$

Step 1: To do this, multiply the bottom numbers together:

$$4 \times 5 = 20$$

This number, 20, can now be used as the bottom number in each fraction, so that they are similar fractions.

Step 2: Change each fraction to have a bottom number of 20.

First, multiply both top and bottom of ¾ by 5 to get the bottom number to 20:

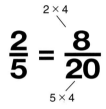

$$\frac{3}{4} = \frac{15}{20}$$

Next, multiply both top and bottom of ⅖ by 4 to get the bottom number to 20.

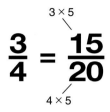

$$\frac{2}{5} = \frac{8}{20}$$

Step 3: Now that we have similar fractions, we can subtract the new top numbers:

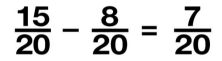

$$\frac{15}{20} - \frac{8}{20} = \frac{7}{20}$$

Now you can see that the answer using the original fractions is:

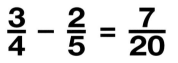

$$\frac{3}{4} - \frac{2}{5} = \frac{7}{20}$$

Remember... Make sure the bottom numbers are the same. When they are, subtract the top numbers, and write the answer over the common bottom number.

Word check

Denominator: The number written on the bottom of a fraction.

Fraction: A special form of division using a numerator and denominator. The line between the two is called a dividing line.

Numerator: The number written on the top of a fraction.

Similar fractions: Fractions with the same denominator.

Book Link... Find out more about subtracting fractions in the book *Fractions* in the *Math Matters!* set.

Using subtracting to solve equations

By putting word problems into equations, it is often much easier to see what the answer should be. Here are four similar problems that show the idea clearly.

• Freda had some computer games. She added five more games, and then she had 14. How many games did she start with?

Freda's problem is: $\boxed{?} + 5 = 14$

• Harry had 14 games but gave some away until he had only 5 left. How many did he give away?

Harry's problem is: $14 - \boxed{?} = 5$

• Inderjit had 14 computer games. He put all his "driving games" to one side and was left with 5 games. How many driving games did he have?

Inderjit's problem is: $14 - \textbf{driving games} = 5$

• Lai Tun Park has a collection of 14 computer games. He took all the "platform games" out, but he forgot to count how many of them there were. Later, all the platform games were stolen. Lai Tun counted that he had 5 games remaining. How many had been stolen?

Lai Tun Park's problem is: $14 - \textbf{stolen games} = 5$

• Although the questions above may all appear to be different, by setting them out as an <u>equation</u>, we discover they are all the same. They can all be represented by the equation:

$$14 - 5 = \boxed{?}$$

and the value of $\boxed{?}$ is always 9. You can see why on page 43.

To solve all of these equations, we need to remember that an equation still balances if we add the same number to each side or if we subtract the same number from each side.

• To solve Freda's problem, subtract 5 from each side of the equation:

$$\boxed{?} + 5 - 5 = 14 - 5$$
$$\boxed{?} = 14 - 5$$
$$\boxed{?} = 9$$

• To solve Harry's problem, add $\boxed{?}$ to both sides:

$$14 - \boxed{?} + \boxed{?} = 5 + \boxed{?}$$
$$14 = 5 + \boxed{?}$$

Now subtract 5 from both sides:

$$14 - 5 = 5 - 5 + \boxed{?}$$
$$\boxed{9} = ?$$

• To solve Inderjit and Lai Tun Park's problems, add either "driving games" (dg) or "stolen games" (sg) to both sides. For example:

$$14 - dg + dg = 5 + dg$$
$$14 = 5 + dg$$

Now take 5 from both sides:

$$14 - 5 = dg$$
$$9 = dg$$

Remember... If we do the same thing to both sides of an equation, it remains balanced.

What symbols mean

Here is a list of the common math symbols together with an example of how they are used. You will find this list in each of the *Math Matters!* books, so that you can turn to any book if you want to look up the meaning of a symbol.

— Between two numbers this symbol means "subtract" or "minus." In front of one number it means the number is negative. In Latin *minus* means "less."

+ The symbol for adding. We say it "plus." In Latin *plus* means "more."

✕ The symbol for multiplying. We say it "multiplied by" or "times."

= The symbol for equals. We say it "equals" or "makes." It comes from a Latin word meaning "level" because weighing scales are level when the amounts on each side are equal.

$$(8 + 9 - 3) \times \frac{2}{5} = 5.6$$

( ) Parentheses. You do everything inside the parentheses first. Parentheses always occur in pairs.

—, /, and **÷** Three symbols for dividing. We say it "divided by." A pair of numbers above and below a / or – make a fraction, so ⅖ or $\frac{2}{5}$ is the fraction two-fifths.

■ This is a decimal point. It is a dot written after the units when a number contains parts of a unit as well as whole numbers. This is the decimal number five point six or five and six-tenths.

Glossary

Terms commonly used in this book.

Counting: Finding the total in a set of things by giving each item a number one more than the last one used.

Counting back: Finding the difference within a set of things by going back through the set.

Decimal number: A number that contains parts of units as well as whole units. The decimal point is used to separate the units from the parts of a unit.

Decimal point: A dot written after the units when a number contains parts of a unit as well as whole numbers.

Denominator: The number written on the bottom of a fraction.

Difference: The result when one number is subtracted from another.

Digit: The numerals 1, 2, 3, 4, 5, 6, 7, 8, 9, or 0. Several may be used to stand for a larger number. They are called digits to make it clear that they are only part of a complete number. So we might say, "The second digit is 4," meaning the second numeral from the left. Or we might say, "That is a two-digit number," meaning that it has two numerals in it, tens and units.

Dividing line: The line that separates the two number parts of a fraction. It is sometimes written horizontally — and sometimes sloping /.

Equation: A number sentence using the = symbol, telling us that two different ways of writing a number are the same. For example, $2 + 2 = 4$ and $9 - 5 = 4$.

Exchanging: In subtracting, this is the method of taking 1 from the column to the left to use it as 10 at the top of your working column, and adding 1 at the bottom of the left column. *See* Regrouping.

Fact family: A group of related facts about adding and subtracting or about multiplying and dividing.

Flat: A large square representing 100. It can also be made up of ten "longs" put side by side.

Fraction: A special form of division using a numerator and denominator. The line between the two is called a dividing line.

Long: A long shape representing 10.

Minus: Another word meaning "subtract."

Minus numbers: The numbers that fall below zero on a number line (scale). Minus numbers or zero cannot be used for counting, only for measuring things like temperature. Minus numbers are also called negative numbers.

Numerator: The number written on the top of a fraction.

Plus numbers: The numbers that fall above zero on a number line (scale). They are called this to separate them clearly from minus numbers. They are the same as counting numbers. Plus numbers are also called positive numbers.

Regrouping: In subtracting, this is the method of moving 1 from the top of the column to the left to use it as 10 at the top of your working column. *See* Exchanging.

Similar fractions: Fractions with the same denominator.

Single-digit number: A number between 0 and 9.

Subtracting facts: The answers we work out and remember as a result of subtracting one number from another. For example, $12 - 7 = 5$ is a subtracting fact.

Two-digit number: A number between 10 and 99.

Unit: 1 of something. A small, square shape representing 1.

Set index